America's Targeted Killing Policy:
Is it Right? Is it Working?

If another nation cannot or will not take action, we will. And it is an unfortunate fact that to save many innocent lives we are sometimes obliged to take lives – the lives of terrorists who seek to murder fellow citizens.

—John O. Brennan[1]

Assistant to President Obama for Homeland Security and Counterterrorism

In response to the attacks on September 11, 2001, the U.S. has been consistently engaged in armed conflict with the Al-Qaeda terrorist group and its associates. The U.S. employs the practice of targeted killing as part of a multi-pronged approach to defeat Al-Qaeda. Although targeted killing is not a new arrow in the U.S.' counterterrorism quiver, it has increasingly become the weapon of choice, has caused notable collateral damage, and has garnered a healthy measure of controversy. Questions swarm regarding the policy's legality, justness, and efficacy, especially with respect to its use outside of 'hot' battlefields such as in Pakistan, Yemen, and Somalia.

Can the U.S. continue the practice of targeted killing to effectively battle terrorism and concurrently maintain the moral high ground in the world's eyes? While it is not clear cut, a reasonable examination of international law and contemporary just war theory shows that a measured practice of targeted killing can be morally just and legal. However, eleven years later, the policy's effectiveness at defeating terrorism is less clear. While it has provided short-term tactical and operational gains, it is questionable whether the policy will be strategically effective against terrorism and its roots. The U.S. should continue the practice of targeted killing but in a more limited fashion with greater transparency. The U.S. is setting precedent for making targeted killing a routine tool of warfare and it should set a worthy example in order to prevent abuse by others.

Definition and Current U.S. Policy

An internationally agreed upon definition of targeted killing does not exist. For the purpose of this research the definition offered by the United Nations (UN) Special Rapporteur, Philip Alston, is used: A targeted killing is the intentional, premeditated and deliberate use of lethal force by States against a specific individual(s) who is not in their physical custody.[2] Note that even though armed remotely piloted vehicles (i.e. drones) are the overwhelming method used by both the U.S. military and the Central Intelligence Agency (CIA), lethal force used for targeted killings can come in many other forms: special forces raid, cruise missile, conventional aircraft attack, etc. Also important is that the definition does not clarify whether criminal law or the law of armed conflict governs the practice.

The U.S. is no stranger to the concept of targeted killing and has used it in direct response to threats against its people or interests. In 1986 the U.S. launched an airstrike against Libya's leaders in response to suspected support of terrorism against U.S. interests.[3] Likewise, in 1998 the U.S. launched cruise missiles into training camps in Afghanistan and into a suspected weapons factory in Sudan in response to terrorist attacks on U.S. embassies.[4] In November 2002 the U.S. killed a key Al-Qaeda leader and five others in Yemen with a drone.[5] But these attacks were rare and were typically accompanied by a detailed explanation from the President or other high-level official. This is in stark contrast to the broad justifications the U.S. offers today coupled with the more routine use of the tactic.

Since 2009, the number of targeted killing strikes in Pakistan's Federally Administered Tribal Area (FATA) has increased more than four times. The U.S. launched an estimated 295 strikes killing an estimated 1,700 militants and a disputed number of civilians.[6] Through a series of speeches given by high level officials in 2012, the U.S. contends that the practice of targeted killing in FATA, Yemen, and Somalia is legally permissible under the 2001 Authorization for Use of Military Force (AUMF) Act which authorizes the President to "use all necessary and appropriate force against those nations, organizations and individuals responsible for 9/11."[7] Additionally, the U.S. states that there is nothing in international law that bans targeted killing outside of an active battlefield when the country involved is *unable* or *unwilling* to take action against the threat.[8] Finally, the U.S. believes it is clearly in the right because it is in a state of armed conflict, has the inherent right of self-defense against *imminent* threats, and is in compliance with the principle of proportionality.[9]

Just War Theory and Legal Considerations

There are numerous contentious legal and moral issues that one could explore with respect to targeted killing. For the purposes of this research the following areas of U.S. policy were examined. First, is the self-defense argument sufficient? Can the U.S. be 'at war' with a non-state actor and justify its intent to violate sovereignty if necessary? Second, is the U.S. abiding by the principle of distinction? How is it certain that the individuals are imminent threats and legitimate military targets? Third, is the U.S. exercising proportionality and the doctrine of double effect?

Few would argue against the U.S.' right to self-defense when it launched offensive operations against the Taliban and Al-Qaeda in Afghanistan in 2001, but does the argument hold water eleven years later with respect to the growing targeted killing campaign? According to Brian Orend, international law and the jus ad bellum concept of just cause allow for a country to defend itself with force when victimized by an armed attack.[10] Clearly this was the case after 9/11 when Congress passed the AUMF Act.

Recently, Jeh Johnson, General Counsel for the Department of Defense, stated that the AUMF is the bedrock for the military's legal authority in its current fight against Al-Qaeda.[11]

However, the AUMF specifically cites those actors and organizations who "planned, authorized, committed, or aided" the 9/11 attacks.[12] In light of Osama bin Laden's recent demise and the fact that Khalid Sheik Mohammed, the mastermind of 9/11, and many other top Al-Qaeda leaders have been captured or killed, the main actors responsible for 9/11 have already been brought to justice. Al-Qaeda's core has been badly hurt, but it is not defeated and the fight must continue. Al-Qaeda has dispersed to other areas and is likely to remain a threat against U.S. interests for a long time beyond the shadow of 9/11.[13] But some argue that at this stage in the war, when we are attacking associate groups in Somalia like al-Shabaab who have no ties to 9/11, embracing the AUMF becomes a legal tap dance and should be revised.[14]

Despite weak domestic authorization, the U.S. policy of targeted killing and its war against Al-Qaeda are within the scope of both international law and contemporary just war theory. Nils Melzer, in his book *Targeted Killing in International Law*, found that non-international armed conflict between a State and a non-State actor is recognized by a narrow interpretation of Articles 2 & 3 of the Geneva Convention and recent rulings by the International Court of Justice (ICJ). However he also states that the law as it stands today needs revision with regard to non-State actors.[15] Furthermore, under the law of inter-state force, the ICJ also found that a State can violate the sovereignty of another if the second State consents or if the acting State is responding under the self-defense clause in Article 51 of the UN Charter in response to an attack or imminent threat, and the second State is unwilling or unable to deal with the threat on its own.[16] This finding by the ICJ supports stated U.S. policy with a key point being that before acting pre-emptively, a State must justify the imminence of the threat.

Since the notion of imminent threat proved false in justifying the 2003 Iraq war, the world is understandably reticent when the U.S. purports to invoke the same argument for killing terrorists in countries with which we are not at war. Therefore the U.S. must exercise due diligence to support its case. Michael Walzer, in *Just and Unjust Wars*, identifies three criteria to justify a pre-emptive or anticipatory attack against an imminent threat, to include violating sovereign territory: 1) a manifest intent to injure, 2) a degree of active preparation that makes the intent a positive danger, and 3) a situation where waiting rather than acting greatly magnifies the risk.[17] The second and third points somewhat overlap with the criteria outlined by Alston where he states that the pre-emptive necessity of self-defense must be "instant, overwhelming," and leave "no moment of deliberation".[18] Al-Qaeda has clearly met Walzer's first criteria by its previous acts and stated intentions. The second and third are more subjective, as are Alston's, and difficult to assess except on a case-by-case basis.

With the large spike in targeted killings in the last four years, coupled with an opaque targeting process, several parties have repeatedly questioned whether the U.S. is targeting true "positive dangers" or imminent threats.[19] According to its top counterterrorism official the U.S. is exercising due diligence by examining the most up-to-date intelligence and verifying that a targeted individual's actions register a significant and imminent threat.[20] However, a Department of Justice memo discussing the legality of targeted killing muddied the waters when it said the U.S. does not require "clear evidence that a specific attack...will take place in the immediate future" when considering whether a threat is "imminent" and that the conflict with Al-Qaeda necessitates a "broader concept of imminence."[21] Since few details have been released on individual cases and in light of this ambiguous justification it is particularly difficult to assess whether the U.S. is meeting the self-defense anticipatory requirements.

Similarly, the agent conducting a strike must ensure that the targeted person(s) is a legitimate military target in order to justify it, both ethically and legally, under the law of armed conflict; otherwise it falls beneath the much more restrictive law enforcement paradigm.[22] Complying with this principle of distinction is problematic when dealing with a shadow organization that doesn't wear uniforms and consistently blends and operates amongst civilians. As difficult as it is, distinction must not be overlooked. Even Walzer recognizes that as we are battling terrorists where traditional just war theory becomes murky, the combatant-noncombatant distinction is crucial.[23] Since the U.S. is engaged in a non-international armed conflict, how should the distinction be made? According to Alston, the U.S. can only target individuals that lose their right to immunity because they "directly participate in hostilities".[24] However, the International Committee of the Red Cross (ICRC) finds this interpretation unsatisfactory because it would create parties to armed conflict whose entire armed forces remain part of the civilian population.[25] Thus the ICRC, which conducted a five-year study from 2003-2008 in light of these issues related to modern conflict, stated that it would recognize the equivalent of armed forces for a non-State actor under a new category, distinct from civilians and traditional State armies, called "organized armed groups."[26]

6

Under the ICRC's organized armed group umbrella, a state could legally target an individual if it is a member that holds a "continuous combat function."[27] These are individuals "whose continuous function involves the preparation, execution, or command of acts or operations amounting to direct participation in hostilities."[28] Conversely, individuals who perform a support function such as recruiters, trainers, propagandists, and financiers cannot be targeted because their role does not constitute a continuous combat function.[29] This seems reasonable considering the alternative of opening up the aperture so wide that nearly anyone connected to an organized armed group could be targeted giving a State a near license to kill.

The U.S. edged toward this slippery slope when it announced the targeting in 2009 of 50 Afghan drug lords because of their financial connections to the insurgency. This declaration raised legal doubts by some NATO allies and others in the human rights community.[30] Similarly, the controversial practice of "signature strikes," which targets anonymous individuals that merely "bear the characteristics of Al-Qaeda," also raised suspicions.[31] Ultimately it is the onus of the State to interpret the criteria for membership and combat role in an organized armed group for each individual. Clearly it must be done in good faith with the most reliable information available to ensure the distinction principle is met. In the ICRC's eyes, that determination "remains subject to all feasible precautions and to the presumption of protection in case of doubt" in order to keep non-combatants out of the cross-hairs.[32] Without specific case details it is difficult to conclude whether the U.S. is making a reasonable effort towards this end.

The last ethical considerations for discussion are proportionality and double effect, which are important when targeted killing strikes threaten civilians. Civilian casualties are a hot topic of late, so much so that in October 2012 a UN official, Ben Emmerson, announced that he is opening up an investigation to examine civilian deaths and U.S. targeted killing policies.[33] When civilians are killed, the question of whether rules of warfare were violated always surfaces.

The *jus in bello* version of proportionality requires that only proportionate force be used against legitimate targets. A common version of this rule is: "do not squash a squirrel with a tank."[34] The recent technological advances in airborne weapons, such as smaller size and greater precision, makes these weapons more reasonable to use against individuals than conventional ones. Not surprisingly, the U.S. acknowledges that these advances have allowed it to be much more discriminating.[35] Arguably, a 20 pound warhead on a precision Hellfire missile, the primary weapon on U.S. drones, is a much better option than an unguided 500 pound bomb when targeting an individual; however, it is not as surgical as a lone bullet and can still cause considerable damage. Thus, according to Melzer, the proportionality assessment should be guided by tailored rules of engagement (ROE).[36] Indeed, according to officials, the U.S. implements specific ROE and has called off drone attacks in the past. Plus, the U.S. chose a special forces raid over an airstrike to capture Bin Laden due to the unacceptable risk of collateral damage.[37] Yet in cases where civilian casualties have occurred, were they justified and was the principal of double effect applied?

The doctrine of double effect in essence says that a target can be prosecuted with force that may result in negative consequences, such as civilian casualties or collateral damage, as long as attacking the primary target is morally permissible, and the "good" result is proportionately greater than the "bad."[38] Walzer adds an additional caveat that says if an act will have "evil" consequences then the actor must seek to minimize the "evil" to include "accepting costs to himself."[39] In other words the actor should exercise due care and possibly assume some risk if he is to fight justly. Finally, Orend and Melzer both argue that not only should a specific attack abide by the double effect principle, but that civilian casualties can only be a just consequence if the target prosecuted is connected to victory, meaning a permanent military solution to the problem ultimately ending the conflict.[40]

It is difficult to assess whether double effect has been violated especially given the minimal detailed information about U.S. targeted killings and the vast accounting variability for civilian casualties. A recent study by the Stanford and New York University Law Schools estimated that since 2004 drone strikes have killed 2,562-3,325 total in Pakistan of whom 474-881 were civilians. This equates to an approximate civilian casualty rate of 23%.[41] Other independent reports show that between 138-191 civilians were killed since 2004, but these numbers do not include a number of "unknowns" who were also killed.[42] Yet another report says since 2008 the civilian casualty rate has dropped to around 11%.[43] U.S. officials stated that since 2008 civilian casualties have been in the "single digits."[44] Another U.S. official reported in July 2011 that no non-combatant casualties had occurred in the last year whereas other independent reports showed that between 92-233 civilians perished during the same time frame.[45]

A further complication is how the bodies are counted. For a time the U.S. embraced that any military-age male was considered a "bad guy" and, without positive ID after-the-fact proving otherwise, was not counted as a civilian casualty.[46] Since the majority of recent strikes have taken place in ungoverned regions of Pakistan and

Yemen, the ability to accurately assess who might have been killed other than the primary target is understandably difficult, but that should not be an excuse for presumptive accounting or giving misleading information to support a policy.

Without an accurate body count relative to who was killed and what their perceived threat level or value was, one is hard-pressed to make a reasonable double effect assessment. Even with accurate information, how do you assess how many civilian casualties a high-value Al-Qaeda or militant leader is worth? Although the civilian death rate appears to be on the decline, reports that the number of high value targets killed since 2004 is only 2% of the total number of fatalities raise additional concerns.[47] One could infer that a large majority of those killed did not rise to the level of imminent threat and would not justify the deaths of civilians. A strike that kills a low-level foot soldier and also kills civilians does not pass the test. If true, the statistics also support critics who say the tactic has become an end unto itself and does not support the overall strategic objective.[48] The fact that multiple reports show a substantial number of civilian casualties, coupled with a relatively small number of high-value targets, and a decade-long war that has merely shifted from Pakistan to Yemen and elsewhere, brings into question whether the U.S. is exercising due care in its practice of these *jus in bello* principles. Without clearer data it will remain unanswered.

Effectiveness

The second area of analysis regarding the U.S.' targeted killing policy is whether the practice is effective in the war against Al-Qaeda and if the second and third-order effects are detrimental to the U.S.' strategic goals. The U.S. has stated that its overall goal is to disrupt, dismantle, and destroy Al-Qaeda. So has the tactic contributed positively or negatively to this goal? In the long run has it helped or hurt the U.S.' image and do we still hold the moral high ground?

The policy of targeted killing has yielded tangible short-term results. The ramped-up attacks over the last four years have eliminated several high-value targets, disrupted operational activities, and hurt Al-Qaeda's morale making it difficult to train.[49] The current administration touted that we have protected our homeland from attacks and that Al-Qaeda is "losing badly" requiring them to flee their once-safe havens.[50] A young idealistic fighter who fought in Pakistan professed that the "flower is wilting" and Al-Qaeda's prestige is on the decline.[51] Even though some argue that dead terrorists are quickly replaced with others, the fact is that when you target highly skilled leaders or bomb makers, finding an equally qualified replacement is difficult, which severely hinders the organization.[52] Conversely, while leader decapitation appears to have acute effects, there is little evidence that a prolonged campaign against leadership realizes long-term reduction of terrorist activities, especially with religiously motivated groups.[53] Overall, there is evidence of short-term gains from targeted killing, but what it is less clear is whether it positively contributes to the long-term strategy of eliminating terrorism's root causes.

Further evaluation reveals that the policy potentially counters long-term goals because it breeds instability and increases recruits. The U.S. will continue to yield short-term gains by primarily only employing airstrikes, but without an effective and complementary counterinsurgency campaign, particularly in Pakistan and Yemen, the environment left behind will spur more instability and mistrust, which are key ingredients to producing more terrorists. A recent study by the Middle East Policy Council concluded that strikes in Yemen had a destabilizing effect, much like Pakistan, which led to less governance.[54] This produced more recruits, retaliatory strikes on local governments, and destabilization. Ultimately, the lack of governance creates a vacuum, which is often filled by extremist leaders and organizations. Without a concurrent counterinsurgency strategy to offset these effects, the policy will continue to create conditions favorable to extremism and terrorism. In a nutshell, the policy "removes any trace of a campaign to win hearts and minds."[55]

Similar doubts about the effectiveness of a counterterrorism strategy without a complementary counterinsurgency strategy surfaced during national leader discussions prior to the Afghanistan troop surge in 2011. General Stanley McChrystal, top military leader in Afghanistan, denied that terrorist decapitation alone would be effective in the long-term without a counterinsurgency campaign. Additionally, General David Petraeus, then Commander of U.S. Central Command, also reflected that killing Abu al-Zarqawi, Al-Qaeda's charismatic and competent leader in Iraq in 2006, did not bring peace or stability by itself. It was the accompanying boots on the ground that set the stage for subsequent progress.[56] Finally, General Michael Hayden, then Director of the Central Intelligence Agency, believed that the U.S. would be doing "piecemeal drone strikes forever," and that the goal of defeating Al-Qaeda was not achievable if "facts on the ground" were not changed.[57] While the U.S. continues to prosecute strikes in minimally governed areas in the Middle East without an accompanying counterinsurgency effort, it is difficult to imagine that it will meet its long-term goals when terrorism's roots are left in place.

Another measure that illuminates if a counterterrorism strategy is working is whether the targeted group can grow. Some state that targeted killing alone will only have a fleeting effect and may boost recruiting.[58] For example, Al-Qaeda in Yemen has increased from 300 fighters in 2009 to over 1,000 in 2012 despite several high profile attacks against them.[59] Additionally, drone strikes have replaced the detention center at Guantanamo Bay, Cuba as the terrorist recruiting tool of choice.[60] In 2010, the individuals behind two separate terrorist plots in New York City both cited that part of their motivation was due to drone killings in their homeland.[61] One of them told a judge "when drones hit, they don't see children."[62] Of course terrorist groups have certainly exaggerated civilian deaths to their advantage for propaganda, but it seems clear that the campaign in Yemen has not stopped the growth of Al-Qaeda and brings into question whether the long-term goal of changing the "tide of hopelessness" can be achieved if it continues as is.[63] A sizable targeted killing counterterrorism policy alone does not curb corruption or improve government services and can have the unintended effect of increasing the threat against the U.S. It cannot substitute for the more difficult and costly process of helping "local leaders marginalize militants."[64]

There is also evidence that instability and motivation against the U.S. as a result of drone strikes is on the rise. In Pakistan some charge that the destabilization left behind has created more problems than it has solved.[65] The campaign has produced a "siege mentality" amongst the populace and could give way to a regional insurgency much like the one in 2006 that occurred in Somalia when similar strikes were employed and the extremists' power was actually solidified.[66] Moreover, in Yemen the strikes have had the unintended effect of refocusing the terrorists' aims from against its local Yemeni government toward targets in the U.S.[67]

The current administration, while articulating its visible tactical results, has also subtly questioned targeted killing's contribution to the long-term strategy. Secretary of State Hillary Clinton expressed concern that the focus on targeted strikes was crowding out the broader strategy to stop radicalization, and that President Obama's goal to mend the U.S.-Muslim relationship cannot move forward in light of the controversial tactic.[68] While senior administration officials expressed that these operations are bound to continue at least for another decade with "no clear end" in sight, experts believe targeted killing through drone strikes is yielding undeniable short-term results while obscuring long-term costs.[69] Dennis Blair, Director of National Intelligence until 2010, stated that drone strikes are "politically advantageous," give the "appearance of toughness," play well domestically, but "any damage done to national interest only shows up over the long-term."[70] The long-term costs are hard to predict with any certainty, but if this campaign is to continue for 10+ years then the U.S. cannot overlook the potential damage to its image in the eyes of the citizens it is trying to persuade.

Since 2009 the U.S. has overused the tactic and has only provided limited transparency into the process, both of which are detrimental to the U.S.' image abroad making it tough to maintain the moral high ground. For example, while small segments of the population in FATA do support the strikes, they have become deeply unpopular amongst the wider population and spurred the parliament to vote for an end to the strikes in 2012, which the U.S. continues to ignore.[71] A 2011 Pew poll revealed that 97% of Pakistanis viewed drone strikes negatively, and 73% had unfavorable views towards

14

the U.S.[72] The anti-Americanism brought on by drone strikes is cited as one of the factors that contributed to the recent sharp rise in violence in Pakistan.[73] According to David Rhode, the excessive drone attacks undercut any laudable policy of multilateralism and transparency, and appears to be backfiring in both Yemen and Pakistan.[74] As cited earlier, Pakistan is less stable today than it was in 2008, and Yemen is yielding numerous sharia-based "emirate" safe-havens for terrorists.[75] Foreign leaders have communicated the issue of overuse to the U.S. The Pakistani military chief told Admiral Mike Mullen, then Chairman of the Joint Chiefs of Staff, "after hundreds of drone strikes, how could the U.S. possibly still be working its way through the Top 20 list?"[76] Overuse is not popular at the local and political levels in Pakistan, which will undoubtedly put a strain on future U.S.-Pakistan relations and the U.S.' image.

The U.S. also needs to be concerned about the perception that it uses drone strikes out of convenience versus pursuing the riskier option of capture. Mr. Brennan stated that the U.S. prefers to capture terrorists whenever feasible but that these opportunities are exceedingly rare and targeted killing is used as a last resort option.[77] While some terrorists have been captured by foreign host countries, only one reported high-profile terrorist has been caught outside of Afghanistan or Iraq by the U.S.: Ahmed Warsame of al-Shabaab in Somalia in 2011. Warsame was easily captured in international waters by U.S. special operations forces.[78] Earlier in 2009 however, a similar mission took place in Somalia against Saleh Nabhan, a senior member of Al-Qaeda's East Africa branch. He was tracked and killed in his convoy in a remote part of the desert by U.S. helicopter gunships. Capture was conceivable, the helicopters even landed to pick up some of his remains for DNA purposes, but many surmised that he was killed because the administration did not have a coherent detention policy in light of the political issues surrounding the closing of Guantanamo Bay and the idea of putting terrorists on trial in New York City.[79] When the capture opportunity is lost or avoided, so is the ability to extract valuable intelligence. With only one high-level terrorist in custody, a 2% kill rate on high-value targets, and civilian collateral damage, the U.S. risks appearing to show a strong preference to killing versus capturing because it is not willing to bear any of the associated risks. Members of the U.S. Congress echoed this concern stating that the policy gives the impression of a "take-no-prisoners" approach.[80]

In defense of the kill versus capture decision, launching a capture mission may produce even more negative effects than a direct strike. Dropping special forces into a populated area to capture a terrorist leader might incur more civilian casualties than a drone strike, especially if they have to shoot their way out.[81] Others argue that drone strikes in Pakistan are more just than the alternative of doing nothing and allowing the local population to be brutalized by the Taliban or an abusive and unpopular Pakistani military.[82] Certainly in today's political atmosphere, few in the U.S. have the stomach for new ground campaigns in the Middle East with the possibility of U.S. casualties. So there is an argument for not pursuing capture, but the harder question still remains: should we continue with the strike with intent to kill, and possibly incur civilian casualties, or wait for an opportunity to capture?

Lastly, the U.S.' image of a strident upholder of the rule of law has come under fire as a result of its opaque stance. One of the clear strategic goals of the current administration is to recapture our "moral authority in the world."[83] Ironically, despite its pre-9/11 objections to Israel using targeted killing strikes on Hamas, the U.S. is now clearly leading the charge in using this tactic to fight its own battle against terrorists. Thus the U.S. is setting the precedent for how other nations may use it in the future. However, the policy has been mired in controversy over many things: lack of transparent criteria; conflicting casualty reports; the use of so-called "signature strikes"; and the killing of U.S. citizens authorized via secret justice department memos, all of which negatively effect the U.S.' image and may potentially lead other nations down the slippery slope of applying their own rules to justify their actions.

The administration has attempted to clarify some of the objections.[84] Through speeches they have focused on the legality of the policy and outlined the process of how a person makes the list and how the decision to target is made. But there are little details on results from specific strikes, particularly when it comes to collateral damage. Despite the stated rigorous process, the troubling practice of signature strikes takes away some of the clarity in the U.S.' position. Signature strikes are different from personality strikes in that they target patterns (e.g. young men touting arms) without positive identification.[85] Without clarity on whether the U.S. condones or embraces signature strikes and the corresponding criteria on how they are justified, then doubt of their legality will continue to brew. As David Luban states the "opacity and unaccountability of the drone program are threats to the rule of law."[86]

Further controversy regarding rule of law escalated with the killing of U.S. citizens Anwar al-Awlaki and Samir Khan in Yemen in 2011.[87] The executive branch alone, through internal deliberations, determined that Fifth Amendment rights of due process were followed. These deliberations were captured in a secret communications within the executive branch that caused significant uproar from civil rights groups.

Without judicial or Congressional review it is impossible to verify the legal justification which further hurts the U.S.' goal toward regaining moral authority. In February 2013 the Obama administration finally released some of these secret documents to select members of Congress.[88] This is a positive step forward, for as General Hayden said, "Democracies do not make war on the basis of legal memos locked in a DOJ safe."[89]

The Way Ahead

Targeted killing and drone strikes have value in the war against Al-Qaeda and are likely to stay not only for the U.S. but also for other nations battling similar threats. In order to maximize the tactic's effect, achieve long-term strategic goals, and improve our image, the U.S. should take the following steps when exercising the tactic outside traditional battlefields.

First, the U.S. Congress should revise the AUMF to provide clarity to the long war against Al-Qaeda. The AUMF is eleven years old and is anchored on 9/11. A revision will reinforce that the U.S. is at war against non-state actors and that it will attack them when necessary under the auspices of anticipatory self-defense. This action will eliminate some of the domestic and international conflict regarding the rules of war, combatant status, and when the use of force is appropriate.[90]

Second, complementary to U.S. legislative action, the U.S. should push for revised international law to encompass this modern form of warfare. As argued earlier there is a narrow legal basis for targeted killing in international law but revision is needed with regard to non-state actors.[91] This is a must if the U.S. is to continue the practice and maintain the moral high ground, but more importantly it will set the standard for those nations that follow with their own targeted killing campaigns.

Third, the U.S. must continue to improve its transparency. The U.S. should make public as much of the policy as possible within security constraints, especially with regard to targeting U.S. citizens. If it remains shrouded in secrecy, any attempt to regain moral high ground and legitimacy will be challenging.[92] It appeared as if the current administration was moving towards providing a more codified process anticipating a potential change due to the 2012 election; however it has apparently stalled again.[93] The U.S. should reinvigorate this action. Additionally the U.S. should provide evidence of what occurred on selected strikes: who was killed, collateral damage, etc.[94] In particular, if the U.S. revealed even minimal details on attacks such as those that were done with "just minutes to act" and explained the imminence of the threat and/or value of the target, this would help diffuse the perception of cavalier overuse.[95] Finally, the U.S. should admit when mistakes are made and consider reparations for those who are unduly harmed.

Fourth, to further boost legitimacy, the U.S. should allow some judicial review of strikes after the fact, similar to what Israel has done with their Supreme Court, especially those strikes on U.S. citizens. This practice, coupled with increased Congressional oversight, would involve all elements of government and provide checks on the executive.[96]

Fifth, the U.S. should drop the practice of signature strikes and should not target individuals who are questionable combatants, such as drug lords. The U.S. should provide evidence for how it identifies targets and how it meets the intent of the criteria set forth by the ICRC for organized armed groups. Again this will help remove the stigma that the U.S. makes up the rules to suit its needs and is willing to abide by accepted international norms.

Sixth, the U.S. should minimize the use of this tactic and target only imminent threats and very high-end leaders. The four-fold increase in attacks since 2009 and the commensurate collateral damage has taken its toll on the U.S.' image and needs to be reversed. Unfortunately this is a war on individuals and as such it must be fought up close and personal.[97] If escalation is required, the U.S. should consider a concurrent U.S.-led or U.S.-supported counterinsurgency strategy in order to stem recruitment and stop deterioration of security conditions on the ground.

Finally, if there is any doubt that an attack may cause civilian casualties, and capture is not an option, then the U.S. should wait for another opportunity. Only in the extremely rare case where it is a true imminent threat and waiting is not tolerable should the strike continue, as Mr. Brennan says, to "save many innocent lives." Given the long loiter capability of drones, which allows a target to be tracked for several hours and/or days, there is no excuse for not exercising patience. Even with the host country's consent, a mistake, and the associated collateral damage to the U.S. image, is just too costly.

The implementation of these recommendations will bring moral clarity and improve chances for long-term success. The war on Al-Qaeda and the tactic of targeted killing are just, necessary, and prudent and will likely be around for a while. Since World War II the U.S. has led the international world order and has been admired as a beacon for democracy and rule of law. With the introduction of powerful non-State actors on the anarchic world stage the U.S. must continue to lead diligently on how a nation should justly prosecute a war against this emergent threat, and how it expects others to as well.

Endnotes

[1] John O. Brennan, "The Efficacy and Ethics of U.S. Counterterrorism Strategy," speech, Woodrow Wilson International Center for Scholars, Washington DC, April 30, 2012, http://www.wilsoncenter.org/event/the-efficacy-and-ethics-us-counterterrorism-strategy (accessed February 10, 2013).

[2] Philip Alston, *Report of the Special Rapporteur on Extrajudicial, Summary or Arbitrary Executions, Philip Alston; Addendum, Study on Targeted Killings* (New York, NY: United Nations, Human Rights Council, May 28, 2010), 3.

[3] Nils Melzer, *Targeted Killing in International Law* (New York, NY: Oxford University Press, 2008), 37.

[4] Ibid., 38.

[5] Alston, *Report of the Special Rapporteur,* 4.

[6] Jonathan Masters, "Targeted Killing," *Council on Foreign Relations Online*, April 30, 2012, http://www.cfr.org/counterterrorism/targeted-killings/p9627 (accessed September 20, 2012).

[7] *Authorization for Use of Military Force*, Public Law 107-40, 107th Congress, Joint Resolution (September 18, 2001), 1.

[8] Brennan, "The Efficacy and Ethics."

[9] Eric H. Holder, speech, Northwestern University School of Law, Chicago, IL, March 5, 2012, http://www.justice.gov/iso/opa/ag/speeches/2012/ag-speech-1203051.html (accessed February 10, 2013).

[10] Brian Orend, *The Morality of War* (Ontario, Canada: Broadview Press, 2006), 32.

[11] Jeh C. Johnson, "National Security Law, Lawyers and Lawyering in the Obama Administration", speech, Yale Law School, New Haven, CT, February 22, 2012, http://www.cfr.org/national-security-and-defense/jeh-johnsons-speech-national-security-law-lawyers-lawyering-obama-administration/p27448 (accessed February 10, 2013).

[12] *Authorization for Use of Military Force*, Public Law 107-40.

[13] Greg Miller, "Plan for Hunting Terrorists Signals U.S. Intends to Keep Adding Names to Kill Lists," *The Washington Post Online*, October 23, 2012, http://www.washingtonpost.com/world/national-security/plan-for-hunting-terrorists-signals-U.S.-intends-to-keep-adding-names-to-kill-lists/2012/10/23/4789b2ae-18b3-11e2-a55c-39408fbe6a4b_story.html (accessed November 2, 2012).

[14] Masters, "Targeted Killing."

[15] Melzer, *Targeted Killing in International Law,* 55, 268-9, 277.

[16] Alston, *Report of the Special Rapporteur*, 12, 15.

[17] Michael Walzer, *Just and Unjust Wars* (New York, NY: Basic Books, 1977/2000), 81.

[18] Alston, *Report of the Special Rapporteur*, 15.

[19] Jo Becker and Scott Shane, "Secret 'Kill List' Proves a Test of Obama's Principles and Will," *The New York Times Online*, May 29, 2012, http://www.nytimes.com/2012/05/29/world/obamas-leadership-in-war-on-al-qaeda.html?pagewanted=all (accessed September 20, 2012); Miller, "Plan for Hunting Terrorists."

[20] Brennan, "The Efficacy and Ethics."

[21] U.S. Department of Justice, "Lawfulness of a Lethal Operation Directed Against a U.S. Citizen Who Is a Senior Operational Leader of Al-Qa'ida or An Associated Force," white paper, posted online by NBC News on February 5, 2013, http://msnbcmedia.msn.com/i/msnbc/sections/news/020413_DOJ_White_Paper.pdf (accessed February 18, 2013). This is an unclassified 16-page document that is reported to summarize the legal arguments contained in a series of classified documents.

[22] Melzer, *Targeted Killing in International Law,* xiii.

[23] Michael Walzer, *Arguing About War* (Harrisonburg, VA: Donnelley, 2004), 139.

[24] Alston, *Report of the Special Rapporteur,* 19; Melzer, *Targeted Killing in International Law,* 331. The U.S. initially tried to label terrorists as 'unlawful combatants' after 9/11, but this never gained international legal traction and according to Melzer was unnecessary.

[25] International Committee of the Red Cross (ICRC), "Interpretive Guidance on the Notion of Direct Participation in Hostilities Under International Humanitarian Law," *International Review of the Red Cross* 90, no. 872 (December 2008): 1003.

[26] Ibid., 1004.

[27] Ibid., 1007.

[28] Ibid.

[29] Ibid., 1008; Melzer, 342.

[30] James Risen, "U.S. to Hunt Down Afghan Drug Lords Tied to Taliban," *The New York Times Online*, August 9, 2009, http://www.nytimes.com/2009/08/10/world/asia/10afghan.html (accessed 8 November 2012); for legal argument against see Patrick Gallahue, "Targeted Killing of Drug Lords: Traffickers as Members of Armed Opposition Groups and/or Direct Participants in Hostilities," *International Journal on Human Rights and Drug Policy*, Vol. I (2010).

[31] Micah Zenko, "Reforming U.S. Drone Strike Policies," *Council on Foreign Relations*, Center for Preventative Action, Council Special Report no. 65, January 2013, 12.

[32] ICRC, "Interpretive Guidance," 1009.

[33] Owen Bowcott, " UN to Investigate Civilian Deaths from U.S. Drone Strikes," *The Guardian Online*, October 25, 2012, http://www.guardian.co.uk/world/2012/oct/25/un-inquiry-U.S.-drone-strikes (accessed November 12, 2012).

[34] Orend, *The Morality of War,* 118-9.

[35] Brennan, "The Efficacy and Ethics."

[36] Melzer, *Targeted Killing in International Law,* 362.

[37] David Luban, "What Would Augustine Do: The President, Drones, and Just War Theory," *Boston Review Online*, June 6, 2012, http://www.bostonreview.net/BR37.3/david_luban_obama_drones_just_war_theory.php (accessed September 20, 2012); Brennan, "The Efficacy and Ethics."

[38] Orend, *The Morality of War*, 115.

[39] Walzer, *Just and Unjust Wars*, 154-5.

[40] Melzer, *Targeted Killing in International Law*, 406; Orend, *The Morality of War*, 118.

[41] International Human Rights and Conflict Resolution Clinic at Stanford Law School and Global Justice Clinic at NYU School of Law, *Living Under Drones: Death, Injury, and Trauma to Civilians From U.S. Drone Practices in Pakistan* (September 2012), vi.

[42] Ibid., 45-47.

[43] Peter Bergen, "Drone is Obama's Weapon of Choice," *CNN Online*, September 19, 2012, http://www.cnn.com/2012/09/05/opinion/bergen-obama-drone/index.html (accessed November 12, 2012).

[44] Becker and Shane, "Secret 'Kill List' Proves."

[45] International Human Rights and Conflict Resolution Clinic, *Living Under Drones*, 161.

[46] Becker and Shane, "Secret 'Kill List' Proves."

[47] Bergen, "Drone is Obama's Weapon of Choice."

[48] Daniel Klaidman, *Kill or Capture* (New York, NY: Houghton, Mifflin, Harcourt Publishing, 2012), 118.

[49] Ibid., 118.

[50] Brennan, "The Efficacy and Ethics."

[51] Klaidman, *Kill or Capture,* 270.

[52] Daniel Byman, "Do Targeted Killings Work?" *Foreign Affairs* 85, no. 2 (Mar/Apr 2006), in ProQuest (accessed October 4, 2012).

[53] Jongmi E. Jim, *The Effectiveness of Leadership Decapitation as a Counterterrorism Strategy Against Islamist Terrorist Groups,* Thesis (Washington, DC: Georgetown University, April 16, 2010), 48-49.

[54] Leila Hudson, Colin S. Owens, and David J. Callen, "Drone Warfare in Yemen: Fostering Emirates Through Counterterrorism?" *Middle East Policy Council Online* (Fall 2011), http://mepc.org/journal/middle-east-policy-archives/drone-warfare-yemen-fostering-emirates-through-counterterrorism (accessed December 5, 2012).

[55] Ibid.

[56] Bob Woodward, *Obama's Wars* (New York, NY: Simon & Schuster, 2010), 190.

[57] Ibid., 25.

[58] David Kilcullen and Andrew Mcdonald Exum, "Death From Above, Outrage Down Below," *The New York Times Online,* May 17, 2009, http://www.nytimes.com/2009/05/17/opinion/17exum.html?pagewanted=all (accessed October 4, 2012).

[59] David Rhode, "The Obama Doctrine," *Foreign Policy Online* (March/April 2012), http://www.foreignpolicy.com/articles/2012/02/27/the_obama_doctrine, (accessed October 4, 2012).

[60] Becker and Shane, "Secret 'Kill List' Proves."

[61] Klaidman, *Kill or Capture*, 119.

[62] Becker and Shane, "Secret 'Kill List' Proves."

[63] Klaidman, *Kill or Capture*, 118.

[64] Rhode, "The Obama Doctrine."

[65] Author Not Provided, "Leaders: Drones and the Law; America's Drone Campaign," *The Economist* 401, no. 8754 (October 2011), in Pro Quest (accessed October 4, 2012).

[66] Kilcullen and Exum, "Death From Above." Adding to the siege mentality, one cannot ignore the historical relevance of airstrikes by a foreign entity. The drone strikes in the tribal areas of Pakistan are eerily similar to "air control" methods employed by the British in the 1920s. This undoubtedly resonates with the local populace to see drone strikes as a continuation of colonial-era abuse; also see *Living Under Drones*, 55, for evidence on how the strikes create an environment where much of the population in the tribal regions of Pakistan live in a constant state of fear.

[67] Robert Wright, "Do Obama's Drone Strikes Imperil America?" *The Atlantic Online*, May 31, 2012, http://www.theatlantic.com/international/archive/2012/05/do-obamas-drone-strikes-imperil-america/257879/ (accessed September 20, 2012).

[68] Becker and Shane, "Secret 'Kill List' Proves."

[69] Miller, "Plan for Hunting Terrorists."

[70] Wright, "Do Obama's Drone Strikes Imperil America?"

[71] Bergen, "Drone is Obama's Weapon of Choice."

[72] Rhode, "The Obama Doctrine."

[73] Masters, "Targeted Killing."

[74] Rhode, "The Obama Doctrine."

[75] Hudson, Owens, and Callen, "Drone Warfare in Yemen."

[76] Miller, "Plan for Hunting Terrorists."

[77] Brennan, "The Efficacy and Ethics."

[78] Klaidman, *Kill or Capture*, 238-9.

[79] Ibid., 126-7.

[80] Becker and Shane, "Secret 'Kill List' Proves."

[81] Luban, "What Would Augustine Do?"

[82] C. Christine Fair, "Drone Wars," *Foreign Policy Online*, May 28, 2010, http://www.foreignpolicy.com/articles/2010/05/28/drone_wars (accessed October 4, 2012).

[83] Klaidman, *Kill or Capture,* 14.

[84] Holder, speech, Northwestern University; Brennan, "The Efficacy and Ethics;" Johnson, "National Security Law."

[85] Klaidman, *Kill or Capture,* 49-50, 256; Becker and Shane, "Secret 'Kill List' Proves."

[86] Luban, "What Would Augustine Do?"

[87] Klaidman, *Kill or Capture*, 263-5.

[88] Michael D. Shear and Scott Shane, "Congress to See Memo Backing Drone Attack on Americans," *The New York Times Online*, February 6, 2013, http://www.nytimes.com/2013/02/07/us/politics/obama-orders-release-of-drone-memos-to-lawmakers.html?pagewanted=all&_r=0 (accessed February 18, 2013).

[89] Becker and Shane, "Secret 'Kill List' Proves."

[90] Mark David Maxwell, "Targeted Killing, The Law, and Terrorists: Feeling Safe?" *Joint Forces Quarterly*, no. 64 (1st quarter 2012): 127, 129.

[91] Melzer, *Targeted Killing in International Law,* 55.

[92] This recommendation was offered by the vast majority of the articles researched for this paper and by MAJ Matthew J. Machon, *Targeted Killing as an Element of U.S. Foreign Policy in the War on Terror*, A Monograph (Fort Leavenworth, KS: School of Advanced Military Studies, U.S. Army Command and General Staff College, May 25, 2006), 57.

[93] Becker and Shane, "Secret 'Kill List' Proves."

[94] Fair, "Drone Wars."

[95] Brennan, "The Efficacy and Ethics."

[96] Byman, "Do Targeted Killings Work?"

[97] Walzer, *Arguing About War*, 136-7.

www.ingramcontent.com/pod-product-compliance
Lightning Source LLC
Chambersburg PA
CBHW080802290526

45790CB00008B/3559